What applicants should know

Be prepared for a lengthy time journey, to almost two thousand years ago. You're going to visit the mighty Roman Empire at the height of its power, round about AD 130. The map below shows your destination – the Roman Empire covers an enormous territory, stretching from southern Scotland to the Caspian Sea. All conquered lands send goods and money to Rome, as tribute and taxes. In return, Roman government officials and Roman soldiers are stationed all around the empire, to make sure that it is well-defended and well-run. You'll find that many local leaders are happy to work alongside Roman rulers. But be warned – others remain hostile. One British chieftain has complained: 'What they (the Romans) call empire-building is just plundering, butchering and theft.'

The Roman Empire

at its greatest size (AD 98-117).

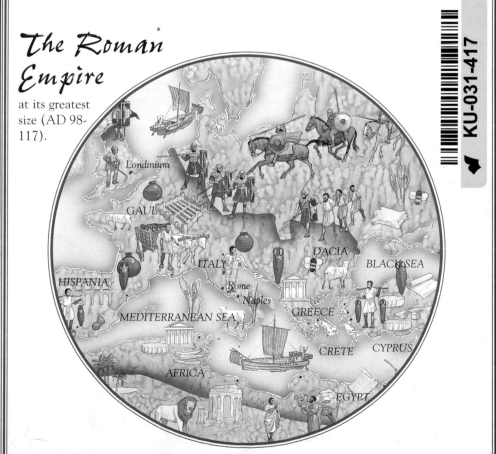

Londinium

GAUL

HISPANIA

ITALY

Rome

Naples

MEDITERRANEAN SEA

AFRICA

DACIA

BLACK SEA

GREECE

CRETE

CYPRUS

EGYPT

Comrades in arms

So you want to join the army! Are you young, male, slim, healthy and at least 1.75m tall? Will you obey orders, fight bravely and work as a member of a team? Do you have good eyesight and hearing? Can you read and write? Most important of all, are you a Roman citizen, born in the Roman Empire? If you can answer 'yes' to all these questions, you may be just the man we are looking for. Even if you are not a Roman citizen, you can still enroll.

How a legion is divided

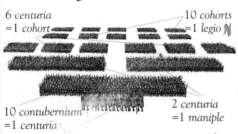

6 centuria =1 cohort

10 cohorts =1 legio

10 contubernium =1 centuria

2 centuria =1 maniple

8 men =1 contubernium (tent-group)

There are about 150,000 regular soldiers in the Roman army, which is divided into legions, each containing about 4,800 men.

Standard-bearers

Could you fight beside tough soldiers like these? The standard-bearers (signiferi) below have been chosen for their bravery to carry each legion's standard in battle. These officers are also responsible for looking after their soldiers' money and savings.

Incedimus XXIV milia per diem ut confinum defendamus.
We walk 24 miles each day to defend the frontier.

Baggage wagon

Auxiliary archers

Auxiliary officers

Standard bearer

Auxiliary centurions

So you want to be a

ROMAN SOLDIER?

Written by
Fiona Macdonald

Illustrated by
Nicholas Hewetson

MACDONALD YOUNG BOOKS

Applying for the job

To make a good impression at your interview, you should be able to speak – or at least understand – the Latin language. It is spoken by army commanders and government officials throughout the Roman Empire, and by other important people, such as travelling merchants and friendly local chieftains, as well. You should also be able to read and write in the Roman way, using the elegant Roman alphabet.

As a regular soldier you need to be able to read lists of army orders, and, while far away on duty, you may want to write letters to comrades far away.

If you have friends or relations who can recommend you for a job in the army, bring a letter of reference from them with you to your interview.

If you cannot read or write, employ a professional scribe to write the letter for you. He should use a stylus (pen) and ink made from soot and oak-gall to write on parchment or thin strips of wood.

Contents

aquila

SPQR

These letters stand for *Senatus Populusque Romanus* which means 'the Senate and people of Rome'.

Legionary or Auxiliary?

There are two different types of soldier in the Roman army – legionaries and auxiliaries. If you're a Roman citizen you can join as a legionary. If you're not a Roman citizen, you'll be recruited as an auxiliary and will be deployed as extra manpower to assist the legionaries, or else as an expert to fight using your own special native techniques.

The carving on this stone coffin (above), shows auxiliary soldiers fighting against tribesmen from Gaul (France).

Army on the march

Picture yourself as a member of this army! How would you fit in? The commander rides in front, followed by bodyguards, musicians and standard-bearers. Then comes a legionary centurion, with a troop of legionary (regular) soldiers, two auxiliary centurions on horseback, their standard-bearer, two auxiliary cavalry officers, auxiliary archers and finally the baggage wagon.

Legionary soldiers

Legionary centurion

Standard bearers

Musicians

Legionary bodyguards

Commander of the Legion

Get kitted out

One day you may depend on your weapons and armour to save your life in battle, so try to get hold of the very best you can. If you're a legionary, the army will provide some of this equipment for you, but if you are an auxiliary you will have to pay for your own clothes and weapons. If you are a cavalry-man, you will have to provide and equip your own horse. Your battle-armour need not be exactly the same as your comrades'. You can choose what you like, so long as your commanding officer approves.

Auxiliary soldiers

Arrows

Chain mail

Sword

Bow

Stabbing sword

Auxiliary soldiers are recruited from many different lands. This archer comes from the Middle East. Auxiliaries use their own weapons so bring your favourites with you. If you have armour, bring that along too.

Special armour

For special occasions, like cavalry displays or festival parades, officers and their men wear beautiful ceremonial armour. They also stage cavalry charges and mock battles, using weapons with wooden, not iron, tips.

Diciplina exercitus Romani tam fevox quam bellum est.

The discipline of the Roman army is as fierce as war.

Shield

Your shield (*scutum*) should be made from strips of wood, glued together and covered with leather or felt. The most useful shape is a curved oblong, about one metre high. This will cover the most vulnerable parts of your body.

Special horse armour

Horses taking part in cavalry displays are also dressed to look their best. Bronze eye shields and metal or leather masks are the most usual items of horse armour. Horses may sometimes wear metal decorations on their bridles, reins and saddle straps.

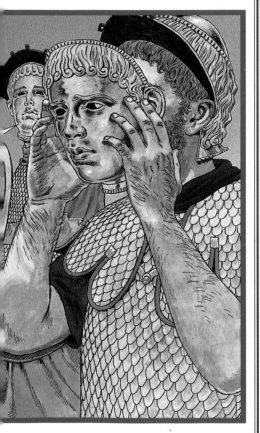

Helmets

The best helmets (*galeae*) are made from iron, and fitted with hinged cheek-pieces on each side of the face and a rigid neck-guard at the back. For comfort and extra protection, they should be padded inside with leather or wool.

Legionary soldier

This is how you'll look as a legionary soldier, fully dressed and ready for battle.

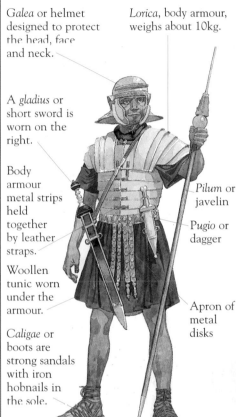

Galea or helmet designed to protect the head, face and neck.

A *gladius* or short sword is worn on the right.

Body armour metal strips held together by leather straps.

Woollen tunic worn under the armour.

Caligae or boots are strong sandals with iron hobnails in the sole.

Lorica, body armour, weighs about 10kg.

Pilum or javelin

Pugio or dagger

Apron of metal disks

Kit

You will have to carry your kit on a wooden pole over your shoulder. Take food, a water bottle, a pot, tools like a spade, a scythe, a mattock and an axe.

Underwear

Wear warm underclothes beneath your tunic. You might also like to wear short pants or loose calf-length trousers and woollen socks.

Army discipline

Now you're sworn-in as a member of the army you'll have to behave properly! The army expects all its soldiers to obey orders instantly and without question. Good discipline in battle is particularly important. If you disobey orders lives may be put at risk. In camp or at the fort, don't let yourself down by arguing with officers or quarrelling. The centurion will punish you, and the others in your tent-group, too. The army believes that men who are very busy, or very tired, won't have the energy to get into trouble! So as well as marching and battle training you'll have to do dirty jobs, called fatigues.

Viaticum

Don't lose these three gold coins! That would get your army career off to a very bad start. They'll be given to you after you have been sworn in as a *viaticum*, to pay for your journey to the army training camp or fort.

Swearing an oath

Remember! For the next 25 years (or until you die in battle) you will be bound by the solemn oath you swore when you were accepted as a new recruit. You must honour the emperor, obey your officers and never desert the army.

Dictum meum pactum.
My word is my bond.

Every morning, at daybreak, you must report to the centurion in charge. He will give orders for jobs to be done today.

Officers in charge

Once you've been sworn in, you'll be under the control of officers (called centurions) who are in charge of army discipline. They are tough, brave soldiers who began their careers as ordinary soldiers like you.

If you've overslept, check the duty rota. You will find your name written there, with the tasks you have to do jotted down beside it.

Fatigues

As a junior soldier, you'll be given all the dirty jobs like cleaning the lavatories, clearing blocked drains, or stoking the bath-house fires. You might also be sent outside the camp to join other soldiers felling timber, quarrying stone and building roads. These tasks will certainly harden your muscles and make you a stronger fighter, but you'll feel exhausted at the end of every day.

Punishments

A terrible punishment awaits all soldiers who rebel or run away. They will be beaten to death by their comrades. If a whole centuria (group of 80 men) disobeys orders, then it will be decimated. This means one in every ten men will be killed.

11

Learning new skills

The army will train you thoroughly. By the end of your first year you'll be a skilled fighter. But don't expect to start weapons training straight away! You won't be allowed near the training ground until you've completed an intensive marching course, designed to build up your strength and stamina and teach you to behave as a member of a team. If you fail to complete this course, you'll be sent home in disgrace, or put on 'punishment rations' of bread until you succeed. After this, you'll be ready for weapons training every day. You'll also be made to take lots of exercise. Running, jumping and swimming are all good preparation for war. If you're intelligent and eager to learn, the army may also train you in a skill – anything from first-aid and nursing to planning and building new forts. If you're prepared to work and study hard, the army can offer you a rewarding career.

Defence

You'll learn defensive formations like this *testudo* (tortoise). You link shields to form an impenetrable 'shell' above your heads.

Marching all day long

Learning how to march will occupy the first four months of your training. To begin with, you'll learn to keep in step with your comrades by marching on the parade ground. Then you'll be sent on route marches, at first just wearing your uniform, then carrying all your kit.

Et caenum et caenum et plus caeni.
Mud, mud and more mud.

Cooking

Cooking skills will come in handy, especially when you're away from the fort. You won't have regular meals of meat, bread and vegetables provided then. Learn to boil lentils and grains to make soup, or how to soak *buccellata* (dry biscuits) in water to make porridge.

No slacking allowed! Even if your muscles are aching and your feet are covered in blisters, by the end of your training you'll have to cover 36km in five hours, or else face a beating from the centurion. The Roman army must move faster than its enemies, or face defeat.

Et pluviam et pluviam et plurimam pluviam.

Rain, rain and more rain.

Experts

The army needs many different specialists, especially architects, surveyors and engineers. If you do well as an ordinary soldier you might be selected to train as an *immunis* – an expert who is let off routine duties to perform important tasks.

Craftsmen

You might be chosen to train for a craft or trade. Carpenters, stone-masons and bricklayers are kept busy building forts. If you qualify you'll do this work and ordinary soldiers will do the labouring jobs.

Learning to fight

At daily weapons training, you'll learn how to fight by attacking hefty wooden posts about two metres high. At first you'll use wooden swords and wicker shields. When you've learnt the basic skills you can practise using real weapons.

Where will you live?

As a soldier, you'll have to get used to living in many different places – some cosy and comfortable, others damp and cold, and maybe dangerous, too!

The army provides two types of living quarters. Marching camps are temporary 'tent-cities', built to house legions as they travel or close to important building sites. You probably won't stay there for more than a few weeks at a time. Forts are bigger and more substantial. They are designed as permanent headquarters for legions living and working far away from Rome. They have barracks, kitchens, bath-houses, lavatories, temples, stables and stores, plus a house for the commander.

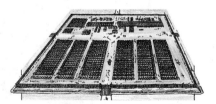

Army camp

The camp is laid out like a small town, with tents in rows. The layout is always the same. This makes it easier for everyone to pitch their tents in a hurry – and for you to find your way back to your own tent, even in the dark. If there are enemies nearby, you'll need to defend the camp by digging ditches and ramparts (earth walls).

Barracks

You might find it rather crowded inside the barracks room (below) at a fort. The eight men in your *contubernium* (tent-group) will have to share a space no bigger than four metres square. Your centurion has a larger room, all to himself, at one end of the barrack block.

Mea galea robiginosa facta est.
My helmet has gone rusty.

Tents

On campaign, you'll live in a *papilio* (tent). These are made of goatskin – it is waterproof and strong, but can be smelly. Use wooden tent pegs to secure it. Cover the ground with straw, bracken, heather or dry grass.

Beds

The bunk-beds are hard and narrow, with rough woollen blankets and mattresses made of straw, but at least you'll be out of the wind and rain. You can't always be sure of that in a tent! You can keep your weapons, armour and kit in the little storeroom next door.

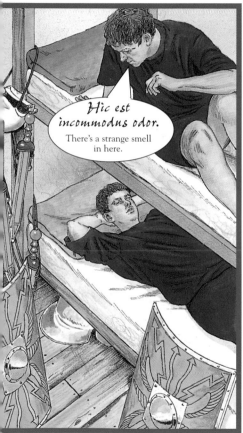

Hic est incommodus odor.

There's a strange smell in here.

A home from home?

Each barrack block inside the fort houses a *centuria* (80 soldiers) and their centurion. Barracks are built of local materials – timber, stone or lath and plaster – and are heated by small stoves in each sleeping room.

Lookouts

Roof with battlements

Trapdoor

Storeroom/ kitchen

Guardroom

Lookouts keep watch from towers built into the fort walls. Each tower has rooms where off-duty men eat and rest. Each fort is surrounded by a ditch, bank and walls. All visitors must report to the sentries at the gates.

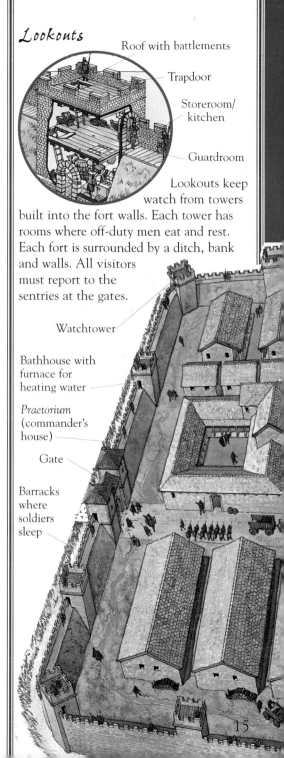

Watchtower

Bathhouse with furnace for heating water

Praetorium (commander's house)

Gate

Barracks where soldiers sleep

15

How much will you earn?

By civilian standards, the army pays quite well.

Milites (ordinary soldiers) earn about 300 denarii each year – almost twice a teacher's salary. But you won't actually receive that amount! The army will keep a lot of it back, to pay for food, clothes, weapons and lodging. They'll also make you save some – they don't want you wasting it on gambling or wine! If you get promoted, you can hope to earn a great deal more. Junior officers earn one-and-a-half times normal pay; senior officers receive double. A top centurion might get 15 times as much as the men he commands. You'll also be rewarded generously when you retire.

Keeping records

The commander of the fort has a staff of well-trained army clerks who keep records of soldiers' pay and all other money spent at the fort.

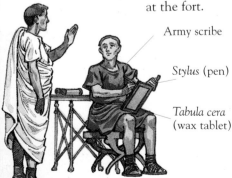

Army scribe

Stylus (pen)

Tabula cera (wax tablet)

Secret store

The best place to keep your savings is in a strongbox in the secret storeroom under the floor of the legion's shrine. The statues of the emperor and gods of war will guard it

The cost of living

You won't be able to afford many luxuries on an ordinary soldier's pay. But if you become a principalis (junior officer) or a centurion, you'll have much more money to spend. Look at the list (right), it gives some prices to guide you.

Purse

Keep money safe in a metal purse like this. It has to be taken off your wrist before you can open it.

Currency

You'll find these Roman coins in use all over the Empire, wherever the army sends you.

1 sestertius = 2 dupondii
1 denarius = 4 sestertii
1 aureus = 25 sestertii

One dupondius can buy two donkeys, but one aureus can buy 100!

Sestertius

Denarius

Dupondius

Aureus

Compendium paene feci ad gladium novum emendum.

I've nearly saved enough for a new sword.

What you can buy

Amphora (huge jar) of wine = 300 sestertii
One sextarius (half litre) of salt = 8 denarii
One libra (half kilo) of pork = 12 denarii
One modius (eight litres) of wheat = 100 denarii
Fashionable shoes = 150 denarii
Woman slave = 2,000-6,000 denarii

Roman alphabet and numbers

You'll see these letters and numbers carved on Roman milestones and inscriptions throughout the Empire:

A, B, C, D, E, F, G, H, I, K, L, M, N, O, P, Q, R, S, T, U, V, X

I = 1	IX = 9	L = 50
II = 2	X = 10	LI = 51
III = 3	XI = 11	XC = 90
IV = 4	XX = 20	XCI = 91
V = 5	XXI = 21	C = 100
VI = 6	XL = 40	CC = 200
VII = 7	XLI = 41	D = 500
VIII = 8	XLIX = 49	M = 1000

17

Join the army and see the world!

In the army you'll have plenty of opportunities to travel, though don't expect your time abroad to be like a holiday! Think of it as an adventure, instead. Troops are always needed to guard the frontiers of the Roman Empire, so be prepared to spend years away from home in distant outposts. These frontier lands are wild, lawless places, where you will fight against local tribes who want to drive the Romans from their lands. You'll see some spectacular scenery, in North African deserts or in forests beside the German river Rhine. But you'll discover that few places have such a pleasant climate as Rome in Italy. Be prepared to shiver in mountain snows, or be burnt by the desert sun.

A typical Roman warship is 45 metres long and 9 metres wide. It carries 600 soldiers, and is crewed by 250 sailors and slaves.

Outposts of the Empire

Hadrian's Wall, on the border between England and Scotland, is one of the coldest places you might be sent to. Soldiers here guard a huge earthwork that stretches for 120km across windy moorland. In winter, it usually snows!

This ballista fires metal bolts

Soldiers ready to defend the ship

16

Transport

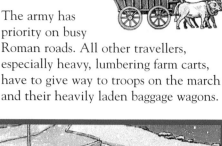

The army has priority on busy Roman roads. All other travellers, especially heavy, lumbering farm carts, have to give way to troops on the march and their heavily laden baggage wagons.

Aegre est mihi! Malim Roma aprica esse.

I feel wretched! I would rather be back in sunny Rome.

Senior officers

Roads and bridges

Top layer of shaped stone slabs

Layer of stone chippings, pebbles or gravel

Layer of stone blocks

Base layer of smooth sand or soil

If you're sent to put down a rebellion on a distant frontier, you'll almost certainly find yourself marching along a well-made Roman road. Be grateful to the men who built it! Roman roads are masterpieces of engineering, carefully planned and surveyed to take the straightest course between important towns.

Soldiers high up in wooden towers on deck keep a lookout for enemy ships. The towers also shelter soldiers from attack.

The warship is powered by men rowing

Is there time for rest and recreation?

Regular duties will keep you busy for most of the day, but the army does allow you to take some time off. Why not explore the surroundings of your fort or camp? Most have a civilian village (*vicus*) nearby, with shops, stalls, taverns, workshops and houses. The inhabitants are friendly – they make a good living by serving Roman customers. And many lonely Roman soldiers fall in love with local girls! The army also organises many other entertainments such as chariot races and gladiator fights on festival days.

Baths

After a long march there's nothing like an afternoon at the baths! You'll emerge clean, refreshed and relaxed. Most forts have their own bath-house, with hot steam-chambers, cold plunge-pools and deep, warm communal baths.

Family life

The army does not allow soldiers to marry, but turns a blind eye to 'unofficial' marriages between soldiers and women who live close to forts and camps. Sadly, you'll find that your duties don't leave you much time for family life.

Quid nodie cenabimus, carissima?
What's for dinner tonight, darling?

Theatre

If you are stationed close to a town, you may be able to go to see plays at the theatre. Which kind of play do you like best? Do you enjoy a good laugh at a comedy, or prefer a heart-stirring tragedy?

For an exciting day out, join the huge crowds watching chariot races in the amphitheatre (bottom).

Mi vir! Gratia dea quod nobis incolumis redisti!

Dear husband! Thank god you've come back safely!

Amphitheatre

It must have taken thousands of hours of soldiers' labour to build this amphitheatre, which stands next to an important Roman fort.

Knucklebones and dice

Gambling is very popular. Will you bet on catching knucklebones (left) or on the fall of the dice (right)? Check dice very carefully before you start to play – they are often 'loaded' (unfairly marked).

Gladiator

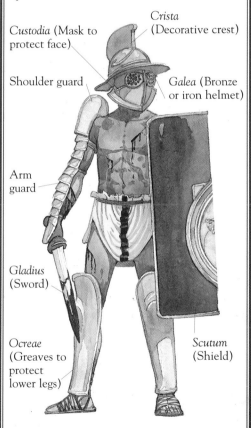

Custodia (Mask to protect face)

Crista (Decorative crest)

Shoulder guard

Galea (Bronze or iron helmet)

Arm guard

Gladius (Sword)

Ocreae (Greaves to protect lower legs)

Scutum (Shield)

Highly paid gladiators (professional fighters), dressed in splendid armour, battle against one another or against wild beasts from the countryside nearby.

What are the dangers of the job?

A soldier's life can be dangerous. There's no point in denying that! Many men die from injuries they receive in battle, or from accidents on army building sites. But remember, life as a farmer, fisherman or professional sportsman can be dangerous as well, and soldiers are stronger and better trained to face risks than men in all these trades. The army makes sure all its men are well fed, with meat and vegetables almost every day. It provides clean water and good sanitation in forts and camps, too. All this means that you will be less likely to die from disease.

If you need an operation

Operations are always risky, but as a soldier you'll receive some of the best medical care in the Roman world. Army doctors use alcohol and herbs as anaesthetics, and know about keeping wounds clean, closing cuts with stitches, amputating damaged limbs and using antiseptics such as turpentine and salt.

Enemies

Always respect your enemy! Don't forget he wants to take your life away from you. Going into battle is the most dangerous thing you'll ever do. But keep calm, remember your training, and use your weapons as you've been taught.

Army doctors can prescribe a range of medicines, often based on herbs. They also have tools for investigating wounds.
a) Chest containing medicines
b) Jars of ointment
c) Probes for examining wounds
d) Spatulas for spreading ointment
e) Sharp knife

Artillery

The Roman army is proud of its big war machines. But *ballistas* (huge crossbows), *onagers* (which hurl rocks) and battering rams can all be very dangerous to the men who operate them, unless handled with care.

Medical equipment

(a)
(b)
(c)
(d)
(e)
(b)

Medical care

Hospitals are an essential part of every fort. They are equipped with beds, operating tables, linen for bandages, and stoves for brewing medicines and preparing drinks.

Lead stopper of jar of 'British Root' medicine, which is believed to cure scurvy.

In battle, you'll see medical staff in the thick of the fighting. They give first-aid to wounded soldiers.

Soldiers who have survived a battle injury often hang thanks-offerings shaped like their wounded limbs in the temple at their fort.

23

Are you officer material?

A s a new recruit you naturally hope that joining the army will lead to a successful career. The men who appointed you hope so too! They like to meet young men who are hard-working and keen. There are two ways to become an officer – by promotion from the ranks of ordinary soldiers, and through noble birth. Because you come from an ordinary Roman family only the first route is open to you. If you are brave and intelligent first of all you'll be promoted to *immunis* (expert) and be trained in one special skill. Then you might become a *tessarius* (commander of a guard troop), and, if you do well, a *signifer* (standard-bearer). If you still show promise, senior officers will appoint you *optio* (deputy centurion) and train you until you reach centurion grade.

A brilliant career

Top army officers are chosen from noble families.

First, they become senators and discuss government policy.

Staff meeting

Every morning, the centurions hurry to the commander's quarters for a daily staff meeting. There they present reports on the men in their units, on how they have arranged

Salvete commilitones!

Good morning, fellow soldiers!

Then they serve as magistrates in a distant province.

They might also be elected as peoples' representative.

the day's duties, and on any sickness or other trouble in the fort or camp. They make plans for any special tasks and order fresh supplies. Everyone agrees on a new secret password (it is changed every day, to prevent enemies entering the camp or fort).

Optatus ades.
You've arrived just on time.

Legionary centurion

Centurions are the backbone of the Roman army. They are strict disciplinarians, and can be harsh and ruthless, but everyone admires them for their bravery and fighting skills.

Galea (Iron or bronze helmet)

Vitis (Vine-wood cane, a sign of rank)

Lorica (Metal breastplate)

Phalera (Medallion with monster's head to drive away harm)

Cingulum (Belt)

Pugio (Dagger)

Gladius (Sword)

Bracae (Knee breeches)

Caligae (Leather boots)

Next, they join the army as *tribunes* (staff officers).

Then promotion to second-in-command.

The best becomes *legatus* (commander of a legion).

A *legatus* might be made governor of a province.

Could you land the top job?

No – not unless you suddenly became emperor, and ruled all the lands conquered by Rome! Because he is head of the Empire, the emperor is also head of the army. Soldiers honour him every day in prayers, and carry a standard bearing his picture into battle with them, to show they are fighting for him, and for all the people of Rome. Some recent emperors, like Trajan (ruled AD 98-117), have been very capable soldiers, and led the army with great success. Trajan conquered Dacia (Romania), Armenia and Mesopotamia (Iraq) and won glory and riches for Rome.
But some past emperors, like Caligula (ruled AD 37-41) and Nero (ruled AD 54-68), were hopeless soldiers, and spent no time with the army at all.

Successful leaders are honoured with a 'triumph'. This is a ceremonial procession through the streets of Rome to receive praise and thanks from the citizens.

Emperor Hadrian

Our present emperor, Hadrian, came to power in AD 117. He has followed emperor Trajan's example, and is a fine army commander. He is especially keen to establish the Roman Empire's frontiers, once and for all, and to defend them from enemy attack.

Booty captured in war

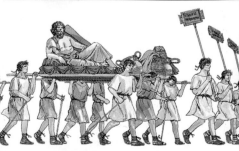

Hadrian has made many visits to the frontier, to inspect and encourage Roman troops serving in distant lands. He even visited northern Britain, which is a very long way from Rome! One day, you may be posted to his vast new frontier fortification there, called Hadrian's Wall.

Veni, Vidi, Vici.
I came, I saw, I conquered!

Monuments

If you go to Rome you should look out for splendid triumphal arches like this. They are built to honour successful commanders and their brave fighting men.

In AD 106, Emperor Trajan decided to build a splendid monument to celebrate his victories in war. It is a tall stone pillar about 30 metres high and is decorated with carvings of Trajan and his soldiers.

Triumphator (person being honoured)

Captured enemies held hostage

What are the long-term prospects?

If you survive in the army for 25 years you can look forward to an honourable retirement. Some soldiers like to return to the land where they were born; others prefer to stay where they last served. Often, they have unofficial wives and children close by. Wherever they settle, few soldiers are idle. Most soldiers are given a retirement gift of land which they can live off by farming. Others might buy a little shop or set up a workshop and make use of the skills they learnt in the army. Even if they die before they reach retirement age, most soldiers still believe that their spirit lives on. Either it has gone to heaven (as some religious teachers say) or else (as many Romans think) it gains strength each time their friends remember them.

Diplomas are often made of bronze, so that they will last for the rest of a soldier's life. Guard your diploma well – it's your passport to years of comfortable retirement.

Soldiers' religion

Many soldiers worship Mithras – a Middle Eastern god who is usually portrayed in the act of sacrificing a bull (right). Mithraism inspires comradeship among soldiers here on earth. But, even more important, it also promises a glorious life after death to men killed in war.

Gratias tibi ago maximas!
Thank you very much indeed!

Diploma award

When you retire from the army, your commanding officer will give you a diploma recording your pension rights. Legionary soldiers normally receive 10 years' pay. This will be enough to set yourself up in business, or buy a little plot of land.